UPDATED EDITION

Guess What!

Student's Book 1B
with eBook

American English

Susannah Reed with **Kay Bentley**

Series Editor: **Lesley Koustaff**

CAMBRIDGE

Contents

		Page
5 My body		**58**
Vocabulary	arms, ears, eyes, feet, hair, hands, head, legs, mouth, nose	60–61
Grammar	I have (a red head and green eyes). ● Do you have (a yellow nose)?	62–63
Story value	Be clean	64
Talk time	*Wash your feet, please.*	65
Animal sounds	*i* ● An iguana with pink ink.	
CLIL: Science	What sense is it?	66–67
6 Food		**68**
Vocabulary	apple, banana, bread, cheese, chicken, egg, juice, milk, orange, water	70–71
Grammar	I like (bananas). ● Do you like (eggs)?	72–73
Story value	Be patient	74
Talk time	*Can I have four apples, please?*	75
Animal sounds	*e* ● An elephant with ten eggs.	
CLIL: Science	Where is food from?	76–77
Review	Units 5–6	78–79
7 Actions		**80**
Vocabulary	climb, dance, draw, jump, paint, play soccer, ride a bike, run, sing, swim	82–83
Grammar	I can (swim)! ● Can you (ride a bike)?	84–85
Story value	Help your friends	86
Talk time	*You can do it!*	87
Animal sounds	*u* ● An umbrella bird can jump.	
CLIL: Math	What's the number?	88–89
8 Animals		**90**
Vocabulary	bird, crocodile, elephant, giraffe, hippo, lion, monkey, snake, spider, zebra	92–93
Grammar	(Elephants) are (big). ● (Elephants) have (long trunks).	94–95
Story value	Respect animals	96
Talk time	*It's small. Respect animals.*	97
Animal sounds	*o* ● An octopus in an orange box.	
CLIL: Science	How do animals move?	98–99
Review	Units 7–8	100–101
My sounds		102–103

5 My body

Guess What!

theme

59

1 🎧 5.01 **Listen. Who's speaking?**

2 🎧 5.02 **Listen, point, and say.**

1 head
2 nose
3 eyes
4 hair
5 ears
6 arms
7 mouth
8 hands
9 feet
10 legs

BIKE CLUB

Find Leo

3 🎧 5.03 **Listen and find.**

4 (5.04) **Say the chant.**

5 (Think) **Look and say the action.**   Number 1. Stamp your feet.

1

2

3

6 🎧 5.06 **Listen, look, and say.**

7 🎧 5.07 (Think) **Listen and say the name.**

i-Lin   i-Tex   i-Zak   i-Con

Grammar fun! ▶

Grammar: *I have a red head and green eyes.*   → Workbook page 50

8 (5.09) **Sing the song.**

9 **Ask and answer.**

Do you have a blue nose and two purple arms?

Yes, I do.

Number 3!

Grammar: *Do you have a yellow nose?*   *Grammar fun!*

10 🎧 5.10 ▶ Story ▶ Listen and watch.

64 Value: Be clean

→ Workbook page 52

11   **Listen and act.**

Animal sounds

12   **Listen and say.**

An iguana with pink ink.

What **sense** is it?

1 🎧 5.15 Listen and say.

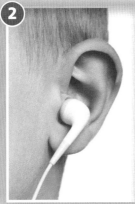

sight   hearing   smell   taste   touch

2 CLIL ▶ Watch the video.

3 Look and say the senses.

Number 1. Sight and touch.   Yes.

Guess What!

Let's collaborate!

OUR **EXERCISE VIDEO**

choose

say

listen and do

move

think   film

6 Food

Look!

Guess What!

theme

69

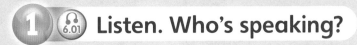

1 🎧 6.01 **Listen. Who's speaking?**

2 🎧 6.02 **Listen, point, and say.**

1 chicken

2 water

3 orange

4 cheese

5 milk

6 egg

7 apple

8 banana

9 juice

10 bread

3 🎧 6.03 **Listen and find.**

Find Leo

→ Workbook page 56

Say the chant.

5 (Think) **Look and find five differences.**

Picture 1. I have chicken.   Picture 2. I have cheese.

6 🎧 6.06 Listen, look, and say.

1

2

7 🎧 6.07 Think Listen and say the name.

> I like chicken and
> I like bananas ...   Kim.

		🍗	🍌	🥛	🥛
Alex		✗	✓	✗	✓
Sasha		✓	✗	✓	✗
Sam		✗	✓	✓	✗
Kim		✓	✓	✓	✗

Grammar: *I like bananas.*   → Workbook page 58

8 (6.09) **Sing the song.**

9 (About Me) **Play the game.**

Number 1. Yellow. Do you like chicken with apples?　　No, I don't.

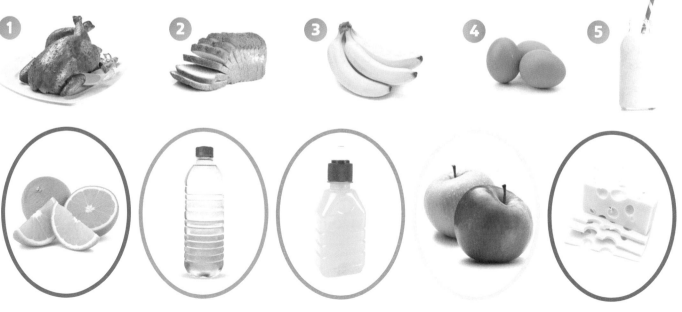

10 6.10 Story ▶ Listen and watch.

74   Value: Be patient

→ Workbook page 60

11   **Listen and act.**

Animal sounds

12 **Listen and say.**

An elephant with ten eggs.

Where is **food** from?

1 🎧 6.15 Listen and say.

plants

1

2

3

animals

4

5

6

2 CLIL ▶ Watch the video.

3 Look and say *plant* or *animal*.

Number 1. Plant.   Yes!

Guess What!

Let's collaborate!

1

2

3

4

like

OUR **FOOD SURVEY**

plants

animals ✓ ✗

ask and answer ?

count

compare

Review Units 5 and 6

→ Workbook pages 64–65

1 Look and say the word.
Number 1. Mouth.

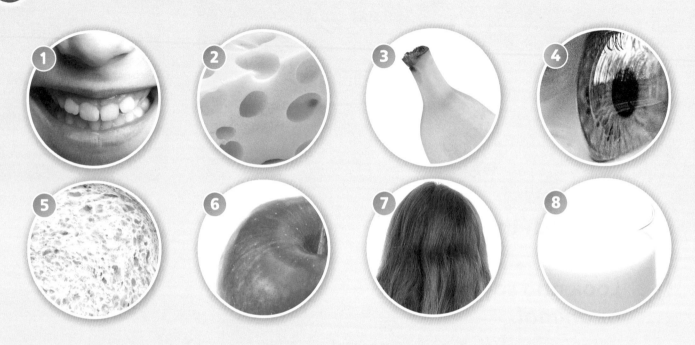

2 🎧 6.16 Listen and say the name.

Tony

Ana

Lily

Ravi

3 Play the game.

Finish

Start

Blue
I don't have (four hands).
I have a (nose).

Green
I like / I don't like
(bananas).

7 Actions

1 🎧 7.01 **Listen. Who's speaking?**

2 🎧 7.02 **Listen, point, and say.**

Come to a **Festival** at the park!

6 ride a bike

5 play soccer

4 climb

3 swim

2 jump

1 run

7 draw

8 paint

9 dance

10 sing

3 🎧 7.03 **Listen and find.**

Find Leo

4 🎧 7.04 Say the chant.

5 Look and match. Then say the action.

Number 1. Green.
Play soccer.

1
2
3
4

6 🎧 7.06 **Listen, look, and say.**

1

2

7 🎧 7.07 **Listen and say the number.** I can run. Six

1

2

3

4

5

6

Grammar fun!

Grammar: *I can swim!* → Workbook page 68

8 7.09 **Sing the song.**

9 (About Me) **Ask and answer.**

Can you
ride a bike?

Yes, I can.

→ Workbook page 69   Grammar: *Can you ride a bike?*

10 🎧7.10 ▶ Story Listen and watch.

86   Value: Help your friends

→ Workbook page 70

11 **Talk Time** Listen and act.

Animal sounds

12 (7.13) Listen and say.

An **umbrella** bird can j**u**mp.

What's the number?

1 7.15 **Listen and say.**

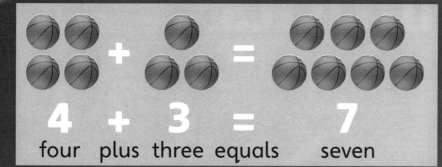

4 + 3 = 7
four   plus   three   equals   seven

8   − 2 =   6
eight   minus two equals   six

Guess What!

2 CLIL ▶ **Watch the video.**

3 **Find the number. Then say the words.**

Five balls plus five balls equals ten balls.

Yes!

① ⚫⚫⚫⚫⚫ + ⚪⚪⚪⚪⚪ = ?

② ⚫⚫⚫⚫⚫⚫ − ⚪⚪⚪⚪ = ?

③ ⚫⚫⚫⚫ − ? = ⚫⚫

Let's collaborate!

think   jump
OUR
SUMMER
CAMP
run
swim
talk
create

8 Animals

Look!

Guess What! theme

1 (8.01) Listen. Who's speaking?

2 (8.02) Listen, point, and say.

1 giraffe

2 monkey

3 elephant   4 bird

5 snake   6 hippo

7 zebra

Africa

8 lion

9 spider

10 crocodile

Find Leo

3 (8.03) Listen and find.

Say the chant.

5 Think **Look and say the animal.**   Number 1. A snake.

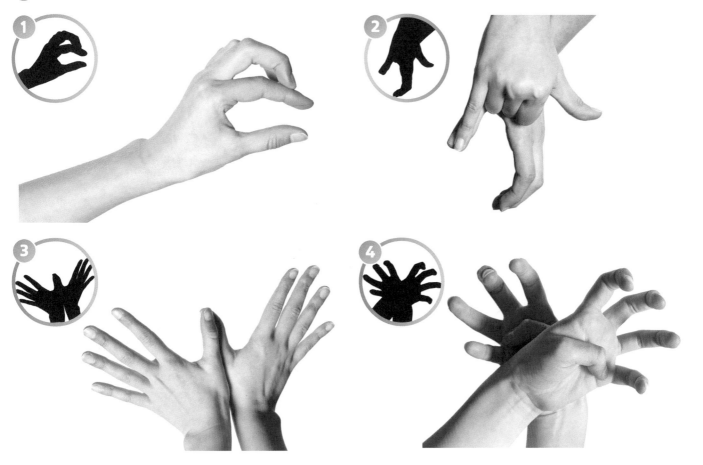

6 🎧 8.06 Listen, point, and say.

long   short

big   small

tall   short

7 🎧 8.07 Listen and say the number.

1

2

3

Grammar fun!

Grammar: *Elephants are big.*   → Workbook page 76

8 (8.08) **Sing the song.**

9 (8.09) **Listen and say *yes* or *no*.**

10 **Look and find five mistakes.**

Giraffes don't have short necks.
Giraffes have long necks.

Grammar: *Elephants have long trunks.*

Grammar fun!

11 8.10 Story ▶ Listen and watch.

96 Value: Respect animals → Workbook page 78

12   **Listen and act.**

Animal sounds

13  Listen and say.

An octopus in an orange box.

How do animals move?

1 🎧 8.15 **Listen and say.**

walk

fly

slither

2 CLIL ▶ **Watch the video.**

3 **Look and say** *walk*, *fly*, **or** *slither*.

A spider can walk. Yes.

Guess What!

1

2

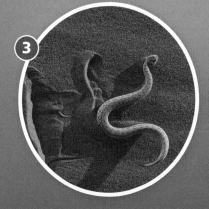
3

4

Let's collaborate!

OUR **ANIMALS** PRESENTATION

discuss

research

present

animals

movement

→ Workbook page 80   CLIL: Science   99

Review Units 7 and 8

1 Look and say the words.

Number 1.
Play soccer.

1

2

3

4

5

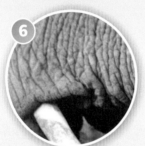
6

7

8

2  Listen and say the number.

1

2

3

4

3 Play the game.

Orange
I can (play soccer).

Green
(Giraffes) have (long necks).

Red
(Birds) are (small).

My sounds

iguana

elephant

umbrella bird

octopus

UPDATED EDITION

Guess What!

Workbook 1B
with Digital Pack

Contents

		Page
Unit 5	**My body**	**48**
Unit 6	**Food**	**56**
Review	**Units 5–6**	**64**
Unit 7	**Actions**	**66**
Unit 8	**Animals**	**74**
Review	**Units 7–8**	**82**
My picture dictionary		**84**
My puzzle		**88**

American English

Susan Rivers

Series Editor: Lesley Koustaff

 CAMBRIDGE

My body

1 **Read and circle the correct word.**

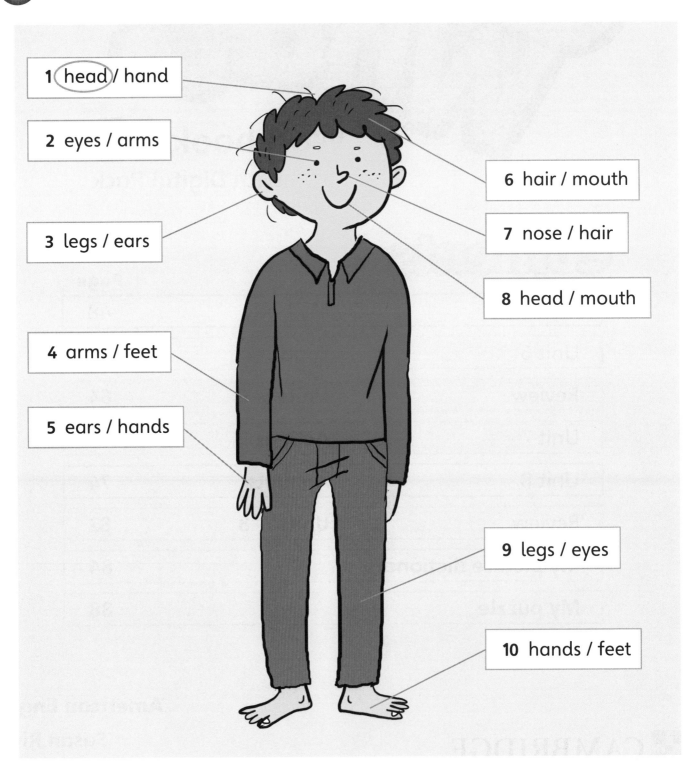

1 (head) / hand

2 eyes / arms

3 legs / ears

4 arms / feet

5 ears / hands

6 hair / mouth

7 nose / hair

8 head / mouth

9 legs / eyes

10 hands / feet

2 🎧 5.05 **Listen and stick.**

1	2	3

4	5	6

3 **Look at the picture. Find and circle the words.**

h	e	a	d	e	p	n
l	e	g	l	a	l	o
h	h	k	o	r	j	s
a	a	e	r	t	y	e
i	r	w	h	a	n	d
r	m	o	u	t	h	n
q	n	v	f	e	e	t

My picture dictionary ➡ Go to page 84: Check the words you know and trace.

4 🎧 5.08 Listen and check ✔.

5 Think What's different? Circle the word.

(eyes) / ears

feet / hands

legs / arms

mouth / nose

6 Look, read, and check ✓.

1

Do you have hair?

 Yes, I do. ✓ No, I don't.

2

Do you have two arms?

Yes, I do. No, I don't.

3

Do you have four legs?

Yes, I do. No, I don't.

4

Do you have one nose?

Yes, I do. No, I don't.

7 (About Me) Draw a robot. Then complete the sentences.

I have _____

_____ .

I don't have _____

_____ .

9 **What's missing? Look and draw. Then stick.**

I'm clean.

a
b
c

10 **Trace the letters.**

An iguana
with pink ink.

11 5.14 **Listen and circle the *i* words.**

 1

 2

 3

 4

What sense is it?

1 **Look, read, and match.**

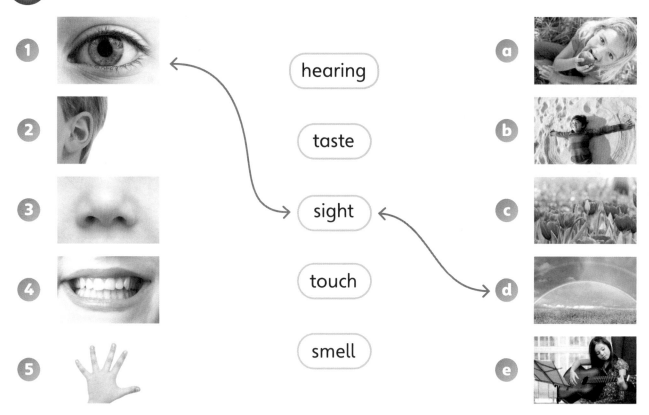

1   hearing

2   taste

3   sight

4   touch

5   smell

a
b
c
d
e

2 **Look and check ✓.**

	👁	👂	👃	😬	✋
	✓				

Evaluation

1 Look, match, and trace. Then read and say.

head

feet

ears

nose

2 What's your favorite part? Use your stickers.

story   song   video

3  Complete the color.

b_u_

Then go to page 88 and color the Unit 5 pieces.

1 Look and write the word.

1

k m l i

milk

2

p e a l p

_____

3

g e g

_____

4

c e h s e e

_____

5

a e w r t

_____

6

a a a n n b

_____

2 Complete the words and match.

1 jui_c_e   2 o _ a n g e   3 b _ e a d   4 c _ i c k _ n

 **a**

 **b**

 **c**

 **d**

3 6.05 **Listen and stick.**

1	**2**
3	**4**

4 Think **Look and write the words.**

~~cheese~~   an apple   juice   bread   water
a banana   an egg   an orange   chicken   milk

We eat ...

1 _cheese_
2 _____
3 _____
4 _____
5 _____
6 _____
7 _____

We drink ...

1 _____
2 _____
3 _____

My picture dictionary → Go to page 85: Check the words you know and trace.

5 🎧 6.08 Listen and check ✓ or put an ✗.

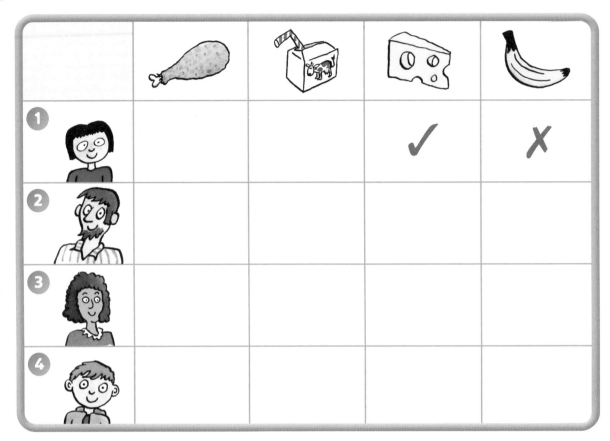

		🍗	🥛	🧀	🍌
1				✓	✗
2					
3					
4					

6 Look, read, and circle.

1  I like / ⟨**don't like**⟩ juice.

2  I **like** / **don't like** oranges.

3  I **like** / **don't like** bread.

4  I **like** / **don't like** water.

5  I **like** / **don't like** apples.

6  I **like** / **don't like** eggs.

7 Look, read, and check ✓.

1

Do you like bread?

✓ Yes, I do. ☐ No, I don't.

2

Do you like eggs?

☐ Yes, I do. ☐ No, I don't.

3

Do you like bananas?

☐ Yes, I do. ☐ No, I don't.

4

Do you like juice?

☐ Yes, I do. ☐ No, I don't.

8 (About Me) Look and answer the questions with *Yes, I do* or *No, I don't.*

1 Do you like chicken?

_____.

2 Do you like milk?

_____.

3 Do you like cheese?

_____.

4 Do you like bananas?

_____.

10 **What's missing? Look and draw. Then stick.**

I'm patient.

11 **Trace the letters.**

An elephant with ten eggs.

12 **Listen and circle the e words.**

1  2  3  4

Where is **food** from?

1 Look and check ✓ or put an ✗.

Plants

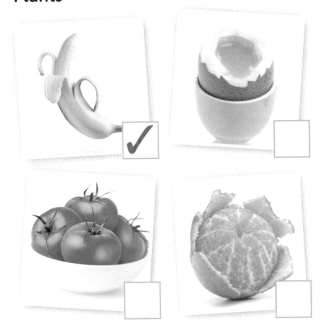

Animals

2 Look, read, and circle.

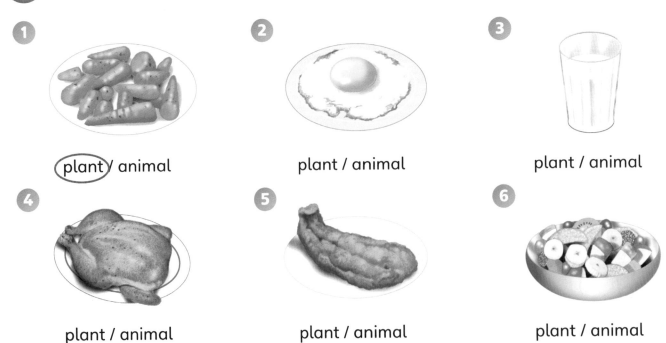

1. plant / animal
2. plant / animal
3. plant / animal
4. plant / animal
5. plant / animal
6. plant / animal

Evaluation

1 Look, match, and write. Then read and say.

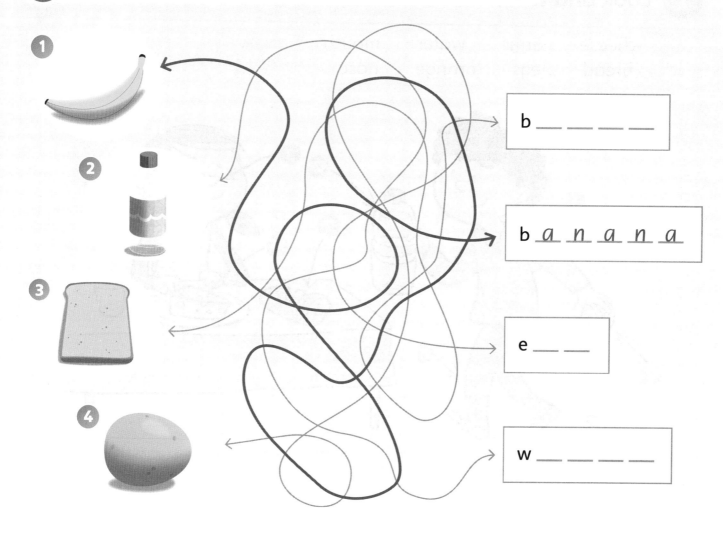

1 b _ _ _ _ _

2 b _a_ _n_ _a_ _n_ _a_

3 e _ _ _

4 w _ _ _ _ _

2 What's your favorite part? Use your stickers.

story   song   video

3 Puzzle Write the color.

p e u l r p _ _ _ _ _

Then go to page 88 and color the Unit 6 pieces.

Review Units 5 and 6

1 Look and write.

cheese   ~~arms~~   water   mouth
bread   legs   orange   nose

1 _arms_ _____   2 _____

3 _____   4 _____

5 _____   6 _____

7 _____   8 _____

2 Read and match.

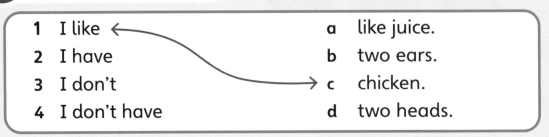

1 I like   a like juice.
2 I have   b two ears.
3 I don't   c chicken.
4 I don't have   d two heads.

3 **Write the question. Then check ✓ .**

1

you / three / Do / have / hands / ?

Do you have three hands?

☐ Yes, I do.   ✓ No, I don't.

2

like / eggs / you / Do / ?

_____

☐ Yes, I do.   ☐ No, I don't.

3

have / two / you / Do / ears / ?

_____

☐ Yes, I do.   ☐ No, I don't.

4

you / Do / milk / like / ?

_____

☐ Yes, I do.   ☐ No, I don't.

7 Actions

1 **Look, read, and circle the word.**

1

swim / (sing)

2

climb / paint

3

dance / draw

4

ride a bike / play soccer

2 **Look at the pictures. Find and circle the words.**

1

2

3

4

5

6

runswimjumppaintclimb(dance)

3 🎧 7.05 **Listen and stick.**

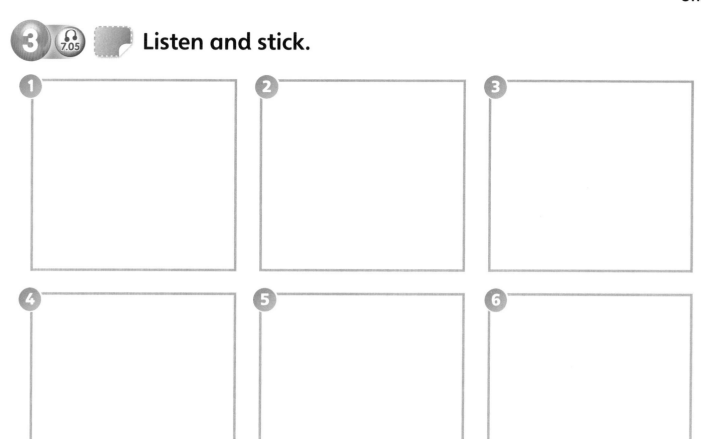

1

2

3

4

5

6

4 Think **Read and circle the object.**

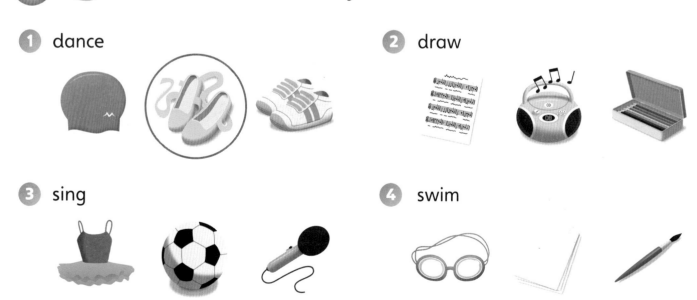

1 dance

2 draw

3 sing

4 swim

My picture dictionary ➔ Go to page 86: Check the words you know and trace.

5 🎧 7.08 **Listen and circle the picture.**

1

2

3

4

6 **Look and write *can* or *can't*.**

1 I __can__ run.

2 I _____ draw.

3 I _____ climb.

4 I _____ dance.

7 Look, read, and check ✓.

1

Can you swim?

[ ] Yes, I can. [✓] No, I can't.

2

Can you jump?

[ ] Yes, I can. [ ] No, I can't.

3

Can you ride a bike?

[ ] Yes, I can. [ ] No, I can't.

4

Can you dance?

[ ] Yes, I can. [ ] No, I can't.

8 (About Me) Complete the chart. Ask three friends and check ✓.

Name			
1 _Me_			
2 _____			
3 _____			
4 _____			

(Can you sing?) (Yes, I can. / No, I can't.)

9 🎧 7.11 Listen and number.

1

10 **What's missing? Look and draw. Then stick.**

I help my friends.

11 **Trace the letters.**

An umbrella bird can jump.

12 (7.14) **Listen and circle the *u* words.**

1  **2**  **3**  **4**

What's the number?

1 **Think and write the answer. Then color.**

1 1 + 1 = | 2 | red **2** 2 + 4 = | | blue

3 3 + 6 = | | orange **4** 10 − 2 = | | purple

5 5 − 2 = | | green **6** 8 − 4 = | | yellow

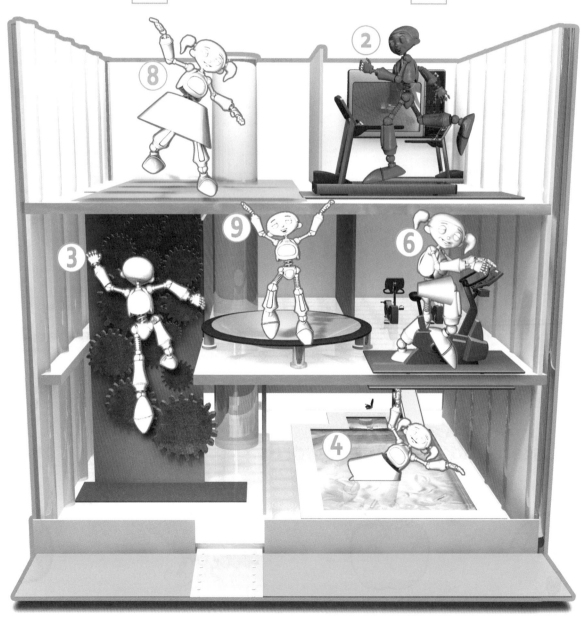

Evaluation

1 Look and write the words. Then read and say.

1 r u n

2 _ _ _ _ _

3 _ _ _ _ _ _

4 _ _ _ _

5 _ _ _ _

6 _ _ _ _ _

2 What's your favorite part? Use your stickers.

story   song   video

3 Puzzle Write the color.

a y r g _ _ _ _ _ _

Then go to page 88 and color the Unit 7 pieces.

8 Animals

1 Look and match.

a crocodile   b giraffe   c spider   d elephant

2 Look and write the word.

1 n l o i

lion

2 b e r z a

_____

3 i d b r

_____

4 o i p h p

_____

5 m y o e k n

_____

6 e a k n s

_____

3 🎧 8.05 📄 **Listen and stick.**

1 | 2 | 3

4 | 5 | 6

4 (Think) **Write the words. Circle the animals with four legs.**

snake   spider   bird   ~~zebra~~   elephant   giraffe   hippo   lion

1 zebra

2

3

4

5

6

7

8

My picture dictionary ➡ Go to page 87: Check the words you know and trace.

5 Look and match the opposites.

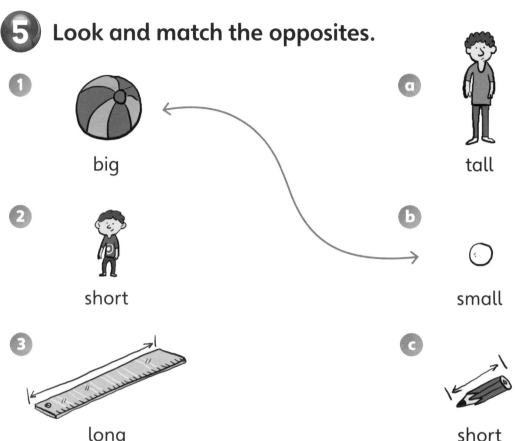

1 big

2 short

3 long

a tall

b small

c short

6 Look, read, and complete the sentences.

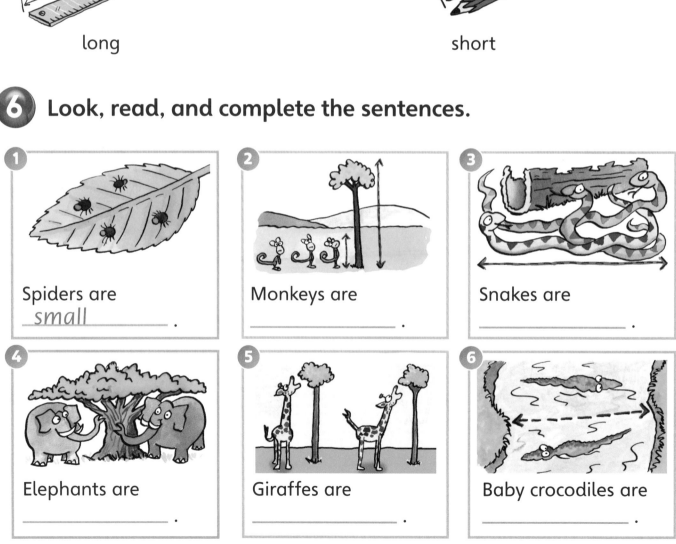

1 Spiders are _small_ .

2 Monkeys are _____ .

3 Snakes are _____ .

4 Elephants are _____ .

5 Giraffes are _____ .

6 Baby crocodiles are _____ .

7 **Look and read. Circle the correct sentences.**

1

Spiders have wings.

2

Elephants have long trunks.

3

Hippos have long necks.

4

Monkeys have long tails.

8 **Look and write.**

big teeth   long tails   ~~small wings~~   long necks   short legs

1 Birds have _small_ _wings_ .

2 Zebras have _____ _____ .

3 Hippos have _____ _____ .

4 Giraffes have _____ _____ .

5 Birds have _____ _____ .

9 **Ask and answer with a friend.**

What are your favorite animals?   Elephants.

1

 ✓

2

3

4

What's missing? Look and draw. Then stick.

I respect animals.

12 Trace the letters.

An octopus in an orange box.

13 8.14 Listen and circle the *o* words.

1  2  3  4

How do **animals** move?

1 Read and complete. Then number the pictures.

slither   ~~walk~~   fly   walk

1 An elephant can ___walk___ .   **2** A snake can _____ .
3 A bird can _____ .   **4** A giraffe can _____ .

a

b

c

d

1

2 Look at Activity 1 and circle the answers.

1 Can a snake fly?   Yes, it can. / No, it can't.
2 Can an elephant walk?   Yes, it can. / No, it can't.
3 Can a bird fly?   Yes, it can. / No, it can't.
4 Can a giraffe slither?   Yes, it can. / No, it can't.

Evaluation

1 **Look and write the word. Then read and say.**

1 _z e b r a_

2 _ _ _ _ _

3 _ _ _ _ _

4 _ _ _ _ _ _ _ _

5 _ _ _ _ _ _ _

6 _ _ _ _

2 **What's your favorite part? Use your stickers.**

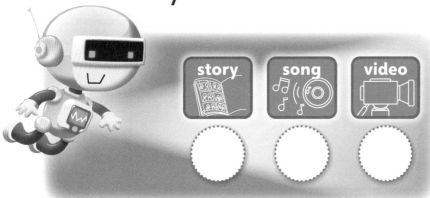

story | song | video

3 Puzzle **Write the color.**

l c k a b _ _ _ _ _ _

Then go to page 88 and color the Unit 8 pieces.

Review   Units 7 and 8

1 Look and write. Then draw number 9.

1 z e b r a

2   a   o c r

3 s a

4 j

5   i   p

6   n   e

7   o   e

8   a n

9

2 Look and write.

soccer   small   long necks   a bike   ~~swim~~

1 Can you ___swim___ ?

2 Birds are _____ .

3 I can play _____ .

4 Giraffes have _____ .

5 I can't ride _____ .

3 Look, read, and circle the words.

1  (Snakes) / **Spiders** are long.

2  I **can** / **can't** sing.

3  Hippos **have** / **don't have** short tails.

4  I can **draw** / **dance**.

5 My body

arms ✓

ears

eyes

feet

head

hair

hands

legs

mouth

nose

6 Food

apple ✓

banana

bread

cheese

chicken

egg

juice

milk

orange

water

7 Actions

 climb ✓

 dance ☐

 draw ☐

 jump ☐

 paint ☐

 play soccer ☐

 ride a bike ☐

 run ☐

 sing ☐

 swim ☐

8 Animals

bird ✓

crocodile

elephant

giraffe

hippo

lion

monkey

snake

spider

zebra

My puzzle

Acknowledgments

Many thanks to everyone in the excellent team at Cambridge University Press & Assessment in Spain, the UK, and India.

The authors and publishers would like to thank the following contributors:

Blooberry Design: concept design, cover design, book design
Hyphen: publishing management, page make-up
Ann Thomson: art direction
Gareth Boden: commissioned photography
Jon Barlow: commissioned photography
Ian Harker: class audio recording
John Marshall Media: "Grammar fun" recordings
Robert Lee, Dib Dib Dub Studios: song and chant composition
Vince Cross: theme tune composition
James Richardson: arrangement of theme tune
Phaebus: "CLIL" video production
Kiki Foster: "Look!" video production
Bill Smith Group: "Grammar fun" and story animations
Sounds Like Mike Ltd: "Grammar Fun" video production

The authors and publishers acknowledge the following sources of copyright material and are grateful for the permissions granted. While every effort has been made, it has not always been possible to identify the sources of all the material used, or to trace all copyright holders. If any omissions are brought to our notice, we will be happy to include the appropriate acknowledgements on reprinting and in the next update to the digital edition, as applicable.

Key: U = Unit.

Student's Book

Photography

The following photos are sourced from Getty Images:

U5: annie-claude/iStock/Getty Images Plus; szefei/iStock/Getty Images Plus; ArtMarie/E+; acilo/iStock/Getty Images Plus; BJI/Blue Jean Images; Robert Daly/OJO Images; MesquitaFMS/E+; Tom Merton/OJO Images; Lucas Ninno/Moment; U6: Jack Hollingsworth/Getty Images; Jose Luis Pelaez Inc/DigitalVision; Wavebreakmedia Ltd/Wavebreak Media/Getty Images Plus; saiko3p/iStock/Getty Images Plus; aliaksei_putau/iStock/Getty Images Plus; Yevgen Romanenko/Moment; Richard Sharrocks/Moment; lacaosa/Moment; milanfoto/E+; happyfoto/E+; antonios mitsopoulos/Moment Open; Jose Luis Pelaez Inc/DigitalVision; stockcam/E+; U7: szefei/iStock/Getty Images Plus; buydeepphoto/iStock/Getty Images Plus; FatCamera/E+; Paul Biris/Moment; Thomas Barwick/Stone; wera Rodsawang/Moment; skynesher/E+; U8: Stuart Westmorland/Corbis Documentary; Elizabeth W. Kearley/Moment; A.Töfke Cologne Germay/Moment; Lintao Zhang/Staff/Getty Images News; Adria Photography/Moment; Istvan Kadar Photography/Moment; Mark Miller Photos/Photodisc; Surasak Suwanmake/Moment; Yannick Tylle/Corbis Documentary; Antagain/E+; Martin Harvey/The Image Bank; BirdImages/E+; blue jean images; Mike Hill/Stone; Life On White/Photodisc; Petr Pikora/EyeEm; stilllifephotographer/Stone; Sally Anscombe/Moment; DENIS-HUOT/hemis.fr; Ableimages/Photodisc; Picture by Tambako the Jaguar/Moment Open; David Muir/Stone; Aldo Pavan/The Image Bank; GEN UMEKITA/Moment; Larry Keller, Lititz Pa./Moment; Picture by Tambako the Jaguar/Moment; Dethan Punalur/Stockbyte; paulafrench/iStock/Getty Images Plus.

The following photos are sourced from other libraries:

U5: Frans Lemmens/Corbis; Pavel L Photo and Video/Shutterstock; Gelpi/Shutterstock; Fisher Lilwin/Tetra Images/Alamy; Federico Rostagno/Shutterstock; Ilya Andriyanov/Shutterstock; Evgeny Bakharev/Shutterstock; miradrozdowski/YAY Media AS/Alamy; Valentina_G/Shutterstock; sbarabu/Shutterstock; foodfolio/foodfolio/Alamy; Liunian/shutterstock; U6: Christian Mueller/Shutterstock; Serg Salivon/Shutterstock; Sea Wave/Shutterstock; ThomsonD/Shutterstock; Chursina Viktoriia/Shutterstock; Sergio33/Shutterstock; Tarasyuk Igor/Shutterstock; Anna Kucherova/Shutterstock; Gino Santa Maria/Shutterstock; Viktor1/Shutterstock; V.S.Anandhakrishna/Shutterstock; Christopher Elwell/Shutterstock; Nattika/Shutterstock; Betacam SP/Shutterstock; Kitch Bain/Shutterstock; Garsya/Shutterstock; aarrows/Shutterstock; R. Fassbind/Shutterstock; colognephotos/Shutterstock; Denis Pogostin/Shutterstock; pattyphotoart/Shutterstock; l i g h t p o e t/Shutterstock; lunamarina/Shutterstock; Zoe Mack/Alamy; Julian Rovagnati/Shutterstock; Anna Moskvina/Shutterstock; ffolas/Shutterstock; PeJo/Shutterstock; xavier gallego morell/Shutterstock; Christian Draghici/Shutterstock; Da-ga/Shutterstock; janinajaak/Shutterstock; andersphoto/Shutterstock; Good Shop Background/Shutterstock; Vaclav Hroch/Shutterstock; Valentyn Volkov/Shutterstock; U7: Juniors Bildarchiv/F314/Juniors Bildarchiv GmbH/Alamy; irin-k/Shutterstock; pics five/Shutterstock; Luminis/Shutterstock; Phovoir/Shutterstock; Pressmaster/Shutterstock; Len44ik/Shutterstock; Monkey Business Images/Shutterstock; R-O-MA/ Shutterstock; silavsale/Shutterstock; Villiers Steyn/Shutterstock; U8: Villiers Steyn/Shutterstock; Don Mammoser/Shutterstock; Maurizio Photo/Shutterstock; Volodymyr Burdiak/Shutterstock; Matt Ragen/Shutterstock; Heiko Kiera/Shutterstock; Jolanta Wojcicka/Shutterstock; Erica Shires/Corbis; Joe McDonald/Corbis; Michael Potter11/Shutterstock; Purcell Pictures, Inc./Alamy; Petra Wegner/Alamy; Solvin Zankl/Nature Picture Library/Corbis; Juniors Bildarchiv BmbH/Alamy; LeonP/Shutterstock.

Workbook

Photography

The following photos are sourced from Getty Images:

U5: Frans Lemmens/Corbis Unreleased; ArtMarie/E+; RusN/iStock/Getty ImagesPlus; Hemera Technologies/AbleStock.com/Getty Images Plus; JessicaPeterson/Brand X Pictures; lostsaga/iStock/Getty Images Plus; iropa/iStock/Getty Images Plus; anskuw/iStock/Getty Images Plus; DigitalVision; U7: Jose Luis Stephens/Getty Images; U8: Joe McDonald/TheImage Bank; Volanthevist/Moment; OwenPrice/iStock/Getty ImagesPlus; Kristian Bell/Moment; brodtcast/Getty Images.

The following photos are sourced from other libraries:

U5: PhotoHouse/Shutterstock; Shane White/Shutterstock; kzww/Shutterstock; Monkey Business Images/Shutterstock; Dmitry Pichugin/Shutterstock; antoniodiaz/Shutterstock; Elena Schweitzer/Shutterstock; AGorohov/Shutterstock; U6: Christian Mueller/Shutterstock; R. Fassbind/Shutterstock; M. Unal Ozmen/Shutterstock; NinaM/Shutterstock; Anna Kucherova/Shutterstock; Tarzhanova/Shutterstock; Efired/Shutterstock; Viktor1/Shutterstock; MaraZe/Shutterstock; U7: Juniors Bildarchiv/F314/Juniors Bildarchiv GmbH/Alamy; U8: Villiers Steyn/Shutterstock.

Front Cover Photography by Dimitri Otis/Stone/Getty Images.

Illustrations

Aphik; Bill Bolton; Chris Jevons (Bright Agency); Joelle Dreidemy (Bright Agency); Kirsten Collier (Bright Agency); Marcus Cutler (Sylvie Poggio); Marek Jagucki; Mark Duffin; Richard Watson (Bright Agency); Woody Fox (Bright Agency); Graham Kennedy; Hardinge (Monkey Feet); Sarah Jennings (Bright Agency).

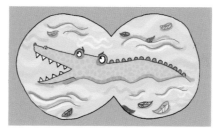